MW01230070

Voices Outside
of Heaven

Identifying Demonic Spirits Operating in Your Life

Kenneth A. Miller

Voices Outside of Heaven: Identifying Demonic Spirits Operating in Your Life.

Published by KAM Global Ministries

Copyright © 2020 Kenneth A. Miller

All rights reserved. No part of this book may be reproduced in any written, electronic, recording, or photocopy, without written permission of the publisher or author. The exception would be in the case of brief quotations embodied in critical articles or reviews and pages where permission is specifically granted by the publisher or author.

Although every precaution has been taken to verify the accuracy of the information contained herein, the author and the publisher assume no responsibility for any errors or omissions. No liability is assumed for damages that may result from the use of information contained within.

Printed in the United States of America.

ISBN – 9781679964220

Table of Contents

Acknowledgement

With a grateful heart, I would like to thank the members and officers of Modern Day Exodus Global Church. I am indeed grateful for them trusting me as a prophetic voice for the last five years.

Also, I would like to thank my family for being sound, supportive voices in my life as I continue to minister the gospel of Jesus Christ.

Dedication

I would like to dedicate this book to those who have been in a war for their heart and mind but did not have the tools to do so victoriously. May this book provide you hope and resources to overcome the demonic barrage coming against you and your family!

If you would like to share your experience with me about this book, kindly email me at kamglobalministries@gmail.com.

Preface

Day after day, there is another force combating the progression of the believers. This force has strategically chosen the human heart and mind as its battleground for this war. These demonic agents are operating outside of the bonds of heaven, secretly influencing people with satanic banter. It is time for us to identify these voices and silence them in the name of Jesus Christ.

Therefore, welcome to **Voices Outside of Heaven: Identifying Demonic Spirits Operating in Your Life!** While writing this particular book, I found that there are many people battling with strange voices in their lives, feeding them knowledge that is wicked and otherworldly. This knowledge seems practical and beneficial to the listeners, but if followed up, it can lead to catastrophic ramifications in that individual's life. To be quite candid, I know the pressures and persuasiveness of these voices because I have personally battled with them. Hence, the urgency to get this resource to you!

Throughout **Voices Outside of Heaven: Identifying Demonic Spirits Operating in Your Life,** I share with you the wisdom that God gave me to silence the satanic voices which tried to lead me on a dark path. These strategies are meant to teach you how to pray, fast and hear accurately the voice of God while shutting down the flow of communication the enemy is trying to establish into your life. It is my hope that you are able to assist others with this truth once you have completed your journey of deliverance.

As of this moment, God is fine tuning your hearing to His frequency, so you will only hear His channel. He is going to debug your spiritual lines, so the enemy can no longer monitor your movements and develop traps along the way.

Most importantly, The Lord shall use you to reach others

who will not have the strength or resolve to fight back against

the teachings of these voices. Be honest and free in prayers,

for the voices that are operating outside of Heaven's laws

shall be silenced today in Jesus' name!

With the Love of Christ,

Kenneth A. Miller

Apostle Kenneth A. Miller, J.P. M.O.
A Prophetic Voice of Deliverance

Introduction

From the beginning of time, there has been an unholy war ensuing behind the scenes. This war has metamorphosed into many different forms over the centuries, but one vehicle of assault has been perfected and consistently exploited. This vehicle of assault is spiritual influence via hearing. These voices outside of Heaven have been influencing people to do things which are contrary to the Law of God and contradict the order He has sovereignly established in the Earth. Due to their covert style of operations, these voices have gone unchallenged, unidentified and even unnoticed. However, it is high time to shine the light on these dark, dishonorable agents and expose them for the purpose of silencing them once and for all. Hence, the coming forth of this book.

Voices Outside of Heaven: Identifying Demonic Spirits Operating within your Life has been birthed by God to divert individuals from the road of obscurity designed to ensnare those who do not know His voice. Written within this book are chapters that delve into the questions many ask about the identification of spirits as well as learning how to distinguish the voice of God from those others voices. Moreover, this book is designed to take an individual through the stages of deliverance straight into developing a personal relationship with God which is unshakable. In addition to teachings and strategies, **Voices Outside of Heaven: Identifying Demonic Spirits Operating within your Life** is equipped with a fasting regime designed to break the cycle of defeatism and tear down demonic strongholds embedded in your life. If you find yourself in a rut and need to identify and combat a specific spirit then you do not have look any further! This book has identified for you more than ten spirits that seek to operate in your life and influence you through satanic omens and rituals disguised as wisdom from on high.

Above all else, we as believers must recognize the authority that we have been given by our Lord and Savior. It is the sole purpose of this book to teach you how to tap into the divine power given to you through the salvation rendered to us by Jesus Christ. This power has the ability to overthrow those spirits seeking dominion over your life while guiding you safely to the Lord. It is at this juncture that we make a turn towards victory and shut down the demonic communications that wish to influence people negatively.

Am I listening to the right voice?

"Verily, verily, I say unto you, He that entereth not by the door into the sheepfold, but climbeth up some other way, the same is a thief and a robber. But he that entereth in by the door is the shepherd of the sheep. To him the porter openeth; and the sheep hear his voice: and he calleth his own sheep by name, and leadeth them out. And when he putteth forth his own sheep, he goeth before them, and the sheep follow him: for they know his voice. And a stranger will they not follow, but will flee from him: for they know not the voice of strangers."

John 10:1 – 5

One of the greatest challenges that many people are faced with is learning how to identify the voices they hear daily. To some, the thought of hearing multiple is strange, but we can see throughout scripture there has always been a fight for the 'ear' of the people. According Romans 10:17, one's faith is built upon what they hear and understanding this principle is the reason for this book. What we hear influences us more than what we see because our ears receive sounds which are interpreted long after the image is gone.

Additionally, what we hear can influence our decision making and emotional stability. This is why people have meetings and conference calls because discussions aid in the understanding of a particular subject matter. What you hear will eventually direct your course. This is the same with children. A child who was motivated and encouraged daily by his or her parents shall experience a natural urge to excel. On the other hand, a child who was degraded and belittled daily will potentially show some signs of dysfunctionality in their everyday behavior. A part of the war going on in our hearts and minds is directly resulting from the things we hear!

Therefore, the purpose of this particular chapter is for you to learn the difference between the voices which will try to persuade you on a daily basis to follow a certain path. Firstly, there are multiple voices operating in our lives whether it be spiritual, sexual or sentimental. However, these voices can be linked to three main influencers: God, your Soul and Satan.

One of the most prominent influencers in your life is the Creator, Jehovah God. This is to be expected due to the fact that He is sovereign and has a destiny for your life that transcends all time and place. However, it is so easy to lose your sensitivity to His voice due to the following factors:

1. **Sin** – the acts that we perform which are contrary to the Word of God creates a separation between us and Him; thus, we lose the ability to properly identify His voice.

2. **Too Many Voices** – allowing people to have more influence our decisions than the Lord will eventually lead to us not really knowing His voice and word.

3. **Lack of a Personal Relationship** – you would never know someone's voice, terms and tone, if you never talked with him or her consistently and intimately. This is the same case with us and God. If we do not spend time with Him, we shall never know His voice and the ways He speaks to us.

4. **Arrogance** – we are so caught up in our personal pursuits and ambitions that we simply disregard anything that does not submit to our agenda.

Even though there are more reasons why we are unable to recognize the voice of God, these four are the primary factors. It is one thing to identify the reasons why you lost your spiritual sensitivity, but let us talk about the 'how' of restoring your ability to hear the voice of the Lord.

In restoring your spiritual hearing, you must step back and silence all of the others voices. This requires fasting and praying. You will know His Voice as you abstain for idle conversations, audible and visual lewdness and excessive busyness. Once you set aside the time and settle yourself, you will be better able to hear His voice. Secondly, the Voice of God can always be traced back to scripture. Hence, the reason why you must dedicate time to read His word. There has been many times I have felt confused and lost, and the only thing that I could have done was read my Bible. A scripture would come to mind then I would read it and it would be exactly what I needed. The 'it came to mind' was the voice of God ministering to my spirit and guiding me to the rivers of living water. A lot of 'my mind told me' was the Holy Spirit nudging us into safety and prosperity!

Therefore, you can even identify the voice of God by the unusual yet profound strategies that comes to your spirit! These kind of instructions are normally simple, weird and sometimes annoying to our flesh. For example, your supervisor lambasted you in front of some customers, and you responded to him with the same fervour. You were only defending yourself, but God knows and sees more than us! Your supervisor walked away crying, and you felt like the mountaineer who finally made it to the summit. Nevertheless, you are having this strange nudging to apologize to him. You ignored it. After severally days, you noticed that your supervisor has not been to work, and 'your mind' tells you to go to your supervisor's home and apologize. Begrudgingly, you make your way to his home. When you arrive, he answered but seemed depressed. You apologized for the incident the other day; he invited you inside to talk. He revealed to you that he just got the news of his divorce before coming to work that day and was gravely distraught. His insults was a result of his inward pain and he also apologized. He admitted that he was battling with suicidal thoughts when you knocked on the door, and your presence was a reminder that he had to continue living! 'Your mind's instructions' resulted in a man being saved from the grip of death. Even though that situation is hypothetical, please know that it is not farfetched. It is a common occurrence, and many do not know that it is God leading them. Be sure to vet your thoughts and those nudges before disregarding them.

Above all else, you will know it is the voice of God by the language. God does not speak like us and normally uses terminology and jargons that are unknown to us. There has been many times that while seeking the Lord for an answer on a particular matter that He said only one word or a short phrase to me. By researching what He said, it resulted in me finding out more than I could have imagined. Try researching or investigating what you are hearing, for you would be surprised by what you find out. In your pursuit to learn how to distinguish between the voices in your life and the voice of God, always remember asking for a confirmation never hurts!

Another proponent seeking to influence your life is Satan. Purposed to keep you living in sin, this voice will always seek to destroy your destiny, kill your purpose and steal time away from your moments of victory. The voice of Satan can sometimes be difficult to discern because of his ability to mix truth in with lies. This is seen in the Garden of Eden with

Eve (Genesis 3) and the Temptation of Christ (Matthew 4:1 – 11). Whenever you are trying to discern the voice of Satan, look out for the following elements:

1. **What did the scriptures say about it?** – If the word of God forbids you to do it then there is no special case to allow for it to be done. For instance, the notion that God desires for us to live, be happy and have fun so it is okay to do whatever you please as long as it is done in moderation. 1 Corinthians 5:6 – 8 stated, *"Your glorying is not good. Know ye not that a little leaven leaveneth the whole lump? Purge out therefore the old leaven, that ye may be a new lump, as ye are unleavened. For even Christ our passover is sacrificed for us: Therefore let us keep the feast, not with old leaven, neither with the leaven of malice and wickedness; but with the unleavened bread of sincerity and truth."* Apostle Paul clearly stated that we

must abstain from the activities we know are sinful even if it seems miniscule. Why? Because sin, just like yeast, starts to expand and develop into a greater demonic work once left uncheck. Beware of instructions that lead you into a deeper pit of sin.

2. **Does it glorify God or the flesh?** – There are many good things that we can do in this world, but the question still remains whether or not it is ultimately fulfilling God's perfect will. Be cautious of doing things that seem productive but was not sanction by God. Take a look at Balaam in Number 22.

3. **Is the intention truly pure?** – There are instances where we are given instructions to carry out, and as we execute them, it further exposes a plot to undermine the perfect will of God. Hence, the instructions or expressed concerns seem good, but the intentions are

impure and soulish. A prime example of such satanic behavior is seen with Bar-Jesus in Acts 13:4 - 12. He earnestly desired the Holy Ghost but for his own nefarious purposes.

The voice of Satan can always be distinguished from the others because its ultimate goal is to lead you away from the perfect will of God.

On the other hand, the voice of the soul is the middle man between the two aforementioned voices. The voice of your soul will always influence you to do what is best for you! It seems simple enough, but what happens when this voice governs your life to the point where sin is the go to answer? For case and point, the soul is comprised of your heart and mind; hence, the reason why the Lord commanded us to love Him entirely with them. (Mark 12:29 - 30) Our soul is the seat of our freewill. Our heart is where our emotional thoughts are birthed, but our mind is where these thoughts are processed and put into action. If either of these sections are not given over the Lord completely, it will eventually open the door for demonic infiltration and influence. Renewing your mind (Romans 12:1 - 2) and cleansing your heart (Psalm 51:10 - 11) are crucial to taming the voice of your soul. In doing so, there are a few things you must do:

- Remove anything out of your life that encourages you to remain focus on the things that do not glorify God

- Disconnect yourself from people whose language and behavior is saturated in negativity and worldliness

- Beware of spending a considerable amount of time in toxic environments

- Spend more time in prayer and studying of the Word

- Listen to more gospel music

- Develop relationships with other born again believers

Your soul requires maintenance and if you do not take the time out to deal with corrosive issues then spiritual holes will begin to form. These holes will lead to the poor management of your spiritual life, and you will find yourself being easily submitted to waywardness.

These three primary voices will always be in your life. However, you must know that only one is truly pure and that is the voice of the Lord. Search intently for His voice. Once you have locked on to His voice, the other voices' influence over your life shall diminish!

Remember This!

1. There are three voices which seek to influence your life: the voice of God, the voice of your soul and the voice of Satan.

2. The voice of God can be identified by the scriptures, its unique strategies as well as its distinct language.

3. The voice of our soul will advise us to do what is best for us, or rather, what is going to please our flesh.

4. The voice of Satan's ultimate purpose is to destroy our destiny, kill our purpose and steal precious moments from our lives.

5. Renewing your mind and cleansing your heart are crucial to your spiritual growth and development.

The War Plan Uncovered

"Another parable put he forth unto them, saying, The kingdom of heaven is likened unto a man which sowed good seed in his field: But while men slept, his enemy came and sowed tares among the wheat, and went his way. But when the blade was sprung up, and brought forth fruit, then appeared the tares also. So the servants of the householder came and said unto him, Sir, didst not thou sow good seed in thy field? from whence then hath it tares? He said unto them, An enemy hath done this. The servants said unto him, Wilt thou then that we go and gather them up? But he said, Nay; lest while ye gather up the tares, ye root up also the wheat with them. Let both grow together until the harvest: and in the time of harvest I will say to the reapers, Gather ye together first the tares, and bind them in bundles to burn them: but gather the wheat into my barn."

Matthew 13:24 – 30

From the beginning of the dawn of time, there has been an unseen war between the Lord and Satan. Satan's main objective is to sully the plans of God for our lives and accumulate evidence which suggest we are unworthy of the blessings of Heaven. In order to fulfill this plan, he enlisted an army to go out into the Earth to kill those who have pledged allegiance to Jesus Christ, destroy the destiny of those who have been called to combat the wiles of the Satanic Kingdom as well as steal glory met for God.

This army is comprised of a three tier cohort. Let us discuss the three tiers individually:

Imps

Imps lower are level demonic spirits that seek access points into our lives such as spiritual open doors, cracks and crevasses. Their main mandate is to create a space large enough so that full pledge demons can gain power and authority over our lives. They use certain tools to fulfil this mandate such as emotional and mental torment, confusion and even stealing our worldly goods. They can be identified in the natural as those small black figures that we see running about in the corner of our eyes or the quick 'open eye' visions of creatures. Due to their limited power and authority, imps can be evicted from your life through concentrated prayer and intensified worship.

Demons

Stronger and more strategic than imps, demons are the second tier of the demonic cohort. These malevolent beings' main goal is to gain control of the life of people so the greater purpose of the satanic kingdom can be fulfilled. Just as the Holy Spirit of God dwells within us and guides us daily so do demons in those who host them. Unlike imps, demons use spiritual laws and principles to gain power and authority over the life of an individual. Moreover, demons use fear, unchecked emotions and would even grant their host access to satanic privileges and blessings to maintain this acquired authority. Depending on the rank and length of time of inhabitation, prayer along with fasting is the only way to command the demon(s) to come out of the person and the region. This is exemplified in Mark 5:1 – 20 and Matthew 17:14 – 21.

Principality

This agent heads the affairs of a demonic cohort and is customarily the demon that gained the most ground in the life of that person or region. The power of this spirit is best exemplified through the constant struggles of that person or region. For example, everybody in the family has a problem with getting married, having full term pregnancies as well as overcoming sexual vices. Hence, all of these isolated problems are associated with an assigned demon that fights against that particular area in the bloodline. In this case, all of the demons would mostly likely be operating under the direction of the Spirit of Perversion. Therefore, it is important for us to understand that all of the demonic spirits within a cohort report to the principality who would advise them on new strategies and tactics to gain more authority and power.

While on the subject, this is how generational curses form! Generational curses form when access is given to demonic spirits in previous generations and they go unaddressed for years; hence, forming a cohort within the bloodline. The only way to dismantle a demonic cohort and subsequently break the generational curses is to follow a three step process:

- Repent of any sins and deeds done by your forefathers. (Deuteronomy 28:15 – 68 / Leviticus 26:14 – 46)

- Turn your life completely over to Jesus Christ and dedicated all of the generations after you to the Lord. (2 Chronicles 7:12 – 16 , Joshua 24:14 -15, Romans 10:9-13)

- Identify the principality in operation and dethrone it through the power of Jesus Christ and the Word of God. (Matthew 4:1-11, Luke 11:14-23, James 4:7-10)

In studying the various scriptures, you will understand that principalities must be challenged with the Word of God and a sound, matured relationship with Jesus Christ. (Acts 19:11-20).

In understanding the different levels of a demonic cohort, you must gain an appreciation for the power of God that is embodied in us upon the confession of faith in Jesus Christ (Romans 10:9 – 13) and subsequent the baptism of water and fire (Acts 2:38 – 39). This embodiment of power comes with a greater access to wisdom and discernment, so you can identify the ploys used by the enemy. Additionally, Jesus Christ expressed in Luke 10 that we have power to overcome all of the devices of satanic forces and overpower their evil advances! As believers, we are challenged to walk in this authority so that we act as agents of freedom in the name of Jesus Christ!

In order to combat the enemy, you must know their strategies of war! Hence, we are going to explore the stages of demonic infiltration and the devices of demonic warfare. Firstly, before a cohort is formally established, there are three stages of demonic infiltration that will take place. The first stage is influence. This is where subtle suggestions and frequent opportunities to sins will take place. For instance, you will find yourself thinking about sexual acts and perverse subjects. This goes on for several days then an attractive person appears and makes advances towards you. It is at this point where the enemy is trying to get you partake in ungodly acts, so the second stage comes into play which is oppression.

Demonic oppression is when the evil forces intensify their warfare because they are trying to gain legal ground in the region and the lives of people. There are three main weapons that will be used during this time: problems, perversion and poverty. Problems are designed to cause an individual to lose faith in God and their spiritual sense of direction while perversion is intended to corrupt the heart and mind (soul) of the individual. Poverty is one of the most interesting of the tools because it is created to redirect the faith and attention of those being targeted to a source outside of the perfect will of God. With these three weapons, the enemy seeks to push the targeted individuals or region into a dark corner and get them to submit his vile desires.

It is while the war is going on that the demonic spirits start to possess areas within the lives of the people or region to create strongholds. This is the beginning of demonic possession. You can tell that someone is demonically possessed by observing the following behaviors:

- Constantly tormented by the things of their past, present and future simultaneously

- Frequent violent, volatile dreams and visions

- Inability to remain stable – mentally, emotionally and socially

- Extreme evasiveness concerning the things of God

- Festering hatred towards born again believers

- Obsession with sexual immorality, mysticism and the black arts

- Lack of self-control, sound mind and spiritual consciousness

- Rebelliousness towards godly leadership (including mockery, defamation and usurpation)

- Exhibits cunningness and manipulation whenever exposed emotionally or spiritually

It is important to learn these points because there are many people living among us today oppressed and possessed by demonic forces, unbeknownst to the general public. For example, the one individual who keeps picking on you at work and goes out of their way to target you can very well be inhabited by forces of darkness. Be vigilant and prayerful before engaging any demonic forces. Moreover, if you are reading this and a few of these are reflected in your behavior, be sure to email me personally at **kamglobalministries@gmail.com.** Your season of deliverance has come!

If you are serving in ministry and have been unable to learn about the process of deliverance, here are few pointers to aid you on your journey:

- Deliverance is salvation in action! This is shown by Luke 4:18 – 21 and John 8:31 – 38. Therefore, Jesus Christ died so that we can be free from the bondage of sin as well as demonic oppression/possession.

- Born again believers, who have a personal relationship with Christ and are filled with His word as well as spirit, have been given the power to expel demon spirits as well as dethrone principalities. This is proven in Mark 3:13 – 15 and Luke 10:19.

- Demons MUST respond to the name of Jesus Christ. Their response is further warranted when that name is called in pure faith and unwavering conviction. Review Philippians 2:5 – 11 and Luke 10:17.

- As you command demonic spirits to leave, be stern, clear and direct! Do not get distracted by what they may say or do. Study Luke 4:33-35 as a reference.

- You must command the demons to go somewhere, and that place would be the Abyss or better known as the pit of hell. Please study Matthew 8:28 – 34.

- After the person or region has been cleansed of the demonic agencies then the Word of God has to be ministered and the understanding developed that they will return to try reclaim their once possessed territory. Review Matthew 12:43 – 45.

- All parties involved must know they are called to a life of holiness and righteousness before the Lord which requires leaving those things of the past behind and making an effort to remain on focused the things of God. Study Galatians 5:16 – 24.

As you are conducting a deliverance session, be mindful of the following signs which act as a confirmation of the expulsion of the demonic forces:

- The need to vomit, spit, urinate and even defecate (please allow the individual[s] to do so)

- Spirits start talking and responding to the prayers

- The passing out of the individual (be sure to monitor the health and wellbeing of the person)

- Weeping that becomes excessive or boisterous

- The person becomes more coherent and genuinely receptive to the Spirit of God

- The region becomes settled and peaceful

There are many other signs to look out for but those are the most common ones. In all things, as a minister of deliverance, you are called to a fasted, prayerful life! Set aside time with God everyday so you are spiritually prepared to handle the darkness that seeks to oppress those around you.

After a person goes through the process of deliverance, there is another journey he or she must embark on quickly. This is the journey of holiness! There are certain acts one must do in order to remain free of demonic infiltration. One must:

- Establish a strong, persistent prayer life

- Continuously shut down any old and new influences of sin in their life

- Remain intently focus on the Word of God

- Find a bible based, Holy Ghost filled church and serve the Lord with gladness

- Remain pure before the Lord with fasting and worship

All of these points will help to build spiritual defences against the future infiltration attempts of the enemy.

As long as we remain focused on the Word of God and His perfect will for our lives, Satan's war plan cannot be fruitful! Isaiah 54:17 bellowed, *"No weapon that is formed against thee shall prosper; and every tongue that shall rise against thee in judgment thou shalt condemn. This is the heritage of the servants of the Lord, and their righteousness is of me, saith the Lord."* This declaration proves to us that standing on the Lord's word shall keep us and with this we know that deliverance is our portion!

Remember This!

1. There are three tiers within a demonic cohort: imps, demons and principalities.

2. Whenever demonic forces are trying infiltrate your life, they will try to influence your daily decisions then they will seek to oppress you with a constant warfare. If given the leeway, they will seek to inhabit and control your life and destiny.

3. In demonic warfare, there are three weapons used to breakdown an individual or region, they are problems (general), poverty and perversion.

4. Deliverance is salvation in action and a ministry unto itself.

5. People who flow in the miracle of power of deliverance are called to a fasted, prayerful life!

6. After undergoing deliverance, you must take several steps to reclaim your destiny and fortify your life against future attacks.

Fasting that facilitates Deliverance

"Is it such a fast that I have chosen?
a day for a man to afflict his soul?
is it to bow down his head as a bulrush,
and to spread sackcloth and ashes under him?
wilt thou call this a fast,
and an acceptable day to the Lord?
Is not this the fast that I have chosen?
to loose the bands of wickedness,
to undo the heavy burdens,
and to let the oppressed go free,
and that ye break every yoke?
Is it not to deal thy bread to the hungry,
and that thou bring the poor that are cast out to thy house?
when thou seest the naked, that thou cover him;
and that thou hide not thyself from thine own flesh?"

Isaiah 58:5 – 7

Throughout biblical history, we see fasting practiced religiously even during the most difficult, tumultuous moments. In the Book of Esther, the young queen called for a fast on her behalf. The fast was intended to ask to the Lord to grant her favor and wisdom to intercede on behalf of the

Jews. That particular fast's stipulations were no food and water for three days. (Esther 4:15 – 16) On other the hand, we see an entire nation abstained from food and drink for the sake of repentance. We saw this happen in the case of Ninevah after Jonah preached a soul riveting message. (Jonah 3) However, fasting today has not been given its rightful mportance in the hearts of modern day believers. This is why we must discuss fasting that brings about change and breakthrough!

Firstly, let us examine what is fasting and its importance. Isaiah 58 gave us a vivid explanation of what is fasting, and it said that it is a time of separation from daily routines and genuinely seeking the Lord's perfect will in reference to our concerns and decisions. This time of seclusion is customarily met with an abstaining from food, drink and unnecessary activities. The scripture went on to even say that a fast can be deemed unworthy or unholy, if we carry on as we are in marketplace or a party. This means our behavior must be reverent, solemn and focused solely on God. Now there are times where we are fasting and have to go amongst people especially if we are working. Jesus Christ taught us in Matthew 6:16 – 18 that we are not to appear as if we are fasting. This means that our behaviour should be cordial, calm and as if it was a regular day, but we are praying reverently onto God. Simply put, fasting is private, personal time with God and it should remain as such! The same principle is applied to corporate fasting; the collective body is sensitive to the Spirit of God and remains solemn before Him. Fasting is intimate, and we should give our undivided attention to the Lord!

In order for the intimacy of fasting to be achieved, we must understand its purpose! Fasting is done for three reasons according to scriptures:

1. Receive an answer from God

2. Intercede on the behalf of another person or group of people

3. Expel demonic forces out a person or region

When done in faith and reverence, fasting amplifies the anointing upon your life and grants you access to a deeper well of power that resides in God. How is this the case you may ask? It is because your spirit man (Job 32:8, 2 Corinthians 4:16, James 2:26) is more open to receive the empowerment of heaven which compels the things of this world, seen and unseen, to submit. Therefore, fasting increases the vessel's ability to contain the power of God so that it can operate unhindered. As you practice fasting on a regular basis, you would find that your spiritual life would greatly improve. To assist with your fasting journey, here are some tips to aid you:

- Ask the Lord to reveal scriptures to you. Studying the Word while fasting increases its retainment and application in your daily life.

- Turn on worship music and spend time 'ministering to the Lord'. Ministering to the Lord refers to being available to do what He has need of you to do. Therefore, when you ascended into a deep, intimate worship, the Lord will speak to you and show you what He requires of you.

- Avoid idle conversations. You would be surprised how a little chit-chat and gossip can leave you into distracted state while fasting. If the conversation is not centered on God and His holy word then it is not necessary at that time.

- Be specific with your prayers. Fasting is a time to really be in tuned to what the Lord has to say; therefore, you need to be direct about your need(s).

Considering the importance that fasting has to the process of deliverance, it is placed on my heart for us to go on a fast for seven days. It is during this fast where the Lord will strengthen you for the deliverance journey and shall break any personal chains that are holding you bond.

This time of fasting comes with daily focus scriptures and journaling pages, so you are able to document your prayers whatever comes to your spirit. The fasting time span will be 7am to 7pm, and you are only to partake in water, hot tea (limited amount of sugar and dairy) and 100% juice during that time. If you are on medication or pregnant, you are encouraged to fast as advised by your physician. Let us begin

our seven day journey of fasting that brings deliverance!

Day One

"Come unto me, all ye that labour and are heavy laden, and I will give you rest. Take my yoke upon you, and learn of me; for I am meek and lowly in heart: and ye shall find rest unto your souls. For my yoke is easy, and my burden is light."

Matthew 11:28 – 30

Journal Entry Date & Time: _____

_____

_____

_____

_____

_____

_____

_____

_____

_____

_____

Day Two

*"Have mercy upon me, O God, according to thy lovingkindness:
according unto the multitude of thy tender mercies blot out my
transgressions.
Wash me throughly from mine iniquity,
and cleanse me from my sin.
For I acknowledge my transgressions:
and my sin is ever before me. Purge me with hyssop, and I shall be
clean:
wash me, and I shall be whiter than snow."*
Psalm 51:1 – 3, 7

Journal Entry Date & Time: _____

_____

_____

_____

_____

_____

_____

_____

_____

Day Three

"And I will bring the third part through the fire,
and will refine them as silver is refined,
and will try them as gold is tried:
they shall call on my name, and I will hear them:
I will say, It is my people:
and they shall say, The Lord is my God."

Zechariah 13:9

Journal Entry Date & Time: _____

_____

_____

_____

_____

_____

_____

_____

_____

_____

_____

Day Four

"And Jesus answering saith unto them, Have faith in God. For verily I say unto you, That whosoever shall say unto this mountain, Be thou removed, and be thou cast into the sea; and shall not doubt in his heart, but shall believe that those things which he saith shall come to pass; he shall have whatsoever he saith. Therefore I say unto you, What things soever ye desire, when ye pray, believe that ye receive them, and ye shall have them."

Mark 11:22 – 24

Journal Entry Date & Time: _____

_____

_____

_____

_____

_____

_____

_____

_____

_____

Day Five

"And he said, Hearken ye, all Judah, and ye inhabitants of Jerusalem, and thou king Jehoshaphat, Thus saith the Lord unto you, Be not afraid nor dismayed by reason of this great multitude; for the battle is not yours, but God's. To morrow go ye down against them: behold, they come up by the cliff of Ziz; and ye shall find them at the end of the brook, before the wilderness of Jeruel. Ye shall not need to fight in this battle: set yourselves, stand ye still, and see the salvation of the Lord with you, O Judah and Jerusalem: fear not, nor be dismayed; to morrow go out against them: for the Lord will be with you."
2 Chronicles 20:15 – 17

Journal Entry Date & Time: _____

_____

_____

_____

_____

_____

_____

_____

_____

Day Six

"And be renewed in the spirit of your mind; And that ye put on the new man, which after God is created in righteousness and true holiness. Wherefore putting away lying, speak every man truth with his neighbour: for we are members one of another. Be ye angry, and sin not: let not the sun go down upon your wrath: Neither give place to the devil."

Ephesians 4:24 – 27

Journal Entry Date & Time: _____

_____

_____

_____

_____

_____

_____

_____

_____

_____

_____

Day Seven

"For what the law could not do, in that it was weak through the flesh, God sending his own Son in the likeness of sinful flesh, and for sin, condemned sin in the flesh: That the righteousness of the law might be fulfilled in us, who walk not after the flesh, but after the Spirit. For they that are after the flesh do mind the things of the flesh; but they that are after the Spirit the things of the Spirit. For to be carnally minded is death; but to be spiritually minded is life and peace."
Romans 8:3 – 7

Journal Entry Date & Time: _____

_____

_____

_____

_____

_____

_____

_____

_____

_____

Exposed then Disposed

"And by the hands of the apostles were many signs and wonders wrought among the people; (and they were all with one accord in Solomon's porch. And of the rest durst no man join himself to them: but the people magnified them. And believers were the more added to the Lord, multitudes both of men and women.) Insomuch that they brought forth the sick into the streets, and laid them on beds and couches, that at the least the shadow of Peter passing by might overshadow some of them. There came also a multitude out of the cities round about unto Jerusalem, bringing sick folks, and them which were vexed with unclean spirits: and they were healed every one."

Acts 5:12 – 16

As we combat the devices of Satan and his cohorts, we must recognize who operates in what role and how that role manifests in our lives. In this chapter, we shall go through some of the most common spirits that plague the people of today. With scripture references and prayer strategies attached, these spirits will soon be exposed and suddenly disposed in Jesus' name!

1. **Spirit of Madness** – this spirit is mainly manifested through emotional and mental instability, overt rebelliousness to the things of God and vengeance. To the average person, an individual oppressed/possessed by this spirit is simply crazy and reckless; however, he or she is being used by demonic forces to wreak havoc and cause fear in the region. The Spirit of Madness can be considered the bulldozer of a demonic cohort. (Mark 5:1 – 5)

   Prayer Strategy: Command the root cause of the spirit's inhabitation to be exposed and healing to come in its stead. Also, declare love and peace into the heart and mind of the individual in Jesus' name.

2. **Spirit of Vengeance** – Birthed from the internalizing of past hurts and pain, the spirit of vengeance takes root in the heart of an individual and develops its powers from there. This spirit is typically manifested through and empowered by unforgiveness, corrupted thinking and negatively influenced perspectives. Unfortunately, the spirit of vengeance is a common agent that influences the generation of today. (Romans 12:17 – 21)

   Prayer Strategy: Decree and declare that all areas infected by hurt, malice and rejection be healed by the blood of Jesus and His holy name. Command the spirit to loosen its grip on the soul of the person and ask the Holy Ghost come in and restore their joy.

3. **Spirit of Infirmity** – As depicted by its name, this spirit is purposed to cause sicknesses and ailments to come up the targeted individual(s) or region. Additionally, the spirit

of infirmity can move throughout bloodlines especially ones where any sacrifices or rituals were performed. Usually accepted genetic/chronic diseases such as hypertension, diabetes and failure of particular organs are manifestations of this spirit. One should be cautious about common yet systematic occurrences where he or she experiences issues with his or her health. (Jeremiah 17:14)

Prayer Strategy: Call the ailment out by name and curse it in the name of Jesus Christ. Command the spirit to leave at once and plead the blood of Christ over all damaged sectors of the body.

4. **Spirit of Poverty** – The weapon of the enemy used to contradict the perfect will of God to prosper His people. This spirit manifests when frequent problems happen which drains the finances especially savings of an

individual. If you find yourself encountering sudden hardships financially, you must seek the Lord to find out what force is being used to combat you. (Deuteronomy 15:7 – 8/Malachi 3:8 – 12)

Prayer Strategy: After searching to find out where the finance leak is in the spirit realm, you are to declare Philippians 4:19 over all areas of your life. You are encouraged to sow a seed into a Christian, Holy Ghost filled ministry which will shift the flow of prosperity back in your favor in Jesus' name.

5. **Spirit of Fear** – this spirit is one of the principalities of the demonic kingdom. It manifests in many different ways and acts as the root of many emotions and behaviors such as depression, anxiety and even suicidal tendencies. (2 Timothy 1:7)

Prayer Strategy: Identify the issues or situations which gave this spirit its authority then command it to be uprooted in the name of Jesus Christ. Ask the Lord to reveal to you the purpose He has ordained for your life then ask Him to guide you accordingly. Fear cannot take root when God is at the helm of your affairs.

6. **Spirit of Perversion** – Another principality in the kingdom of darkness. The spirit of perversion seeks to govern the soul of an individual. The soul, being comprised of the heart and mind, is the perfect place to exact its will. Perversion uses sexual immorality, the distortion of truth and holiness as well as manipulation to establish strongholds in an individual's life. Therefore, beware of the subtle drifting away from the word and principles of God.

Prayer Strategy: Repent of all acts or thoughts that would have given this spirit access to your life. Command every lie and twisted truth to be dismantled in Jesus' name. Speak clarity of your life and recall the word of God into the depths of your soul in Jesus' name.

7. **Spirit of Greed & Gluttony** – One of the most overlooked spirits is greed and gluttony. People who have the need to hoard money, worldly possessions and food to the point of jeopardizing other lives to do so are under demonic influence. (Psalm 10:2 – 3)

   Prayer Strategy: Ask the Lord to give you the strength to develop self-control and dependency on Him.

8. **Spirit of Confusion** – This particular spirit is sent out to torment an individual or region with a plethora of problems including miscommunications and division. When left unaddressed, the spirit of confusion can alter

the perspectives of people and cause them to live in a cycle of defeatism and rejection. (Genesis 11:1 - 9)

Prayer Strategy: Command the voices of darkness to be silent and the voice of God to resound in the atmosphere. Afterwards, decree and declare that every false prophecy and demonic declaration shall not come to fruition in Jesus' name.

9. **Spirit of Pride** - Birthed out of the heart of man and nurtured by demonic agents, pride is one of the attributes the Lord despised greatly. Pride is the belief that one is either better than another or wishes sit in a seat of control to prevent himself or herself from feeling or being subservient. The Spirit of Pride is manifested through arrogance, a controlling complex and false persona of self-sufficiency. (Proverbs 6:16 - 19)

Prayer Strategy: Ask God to grant you to ability to trust others as He guides them. Give Him the glory for all that is done in your life and works. Embrace the humbling moments and ask God to give you the strength to retain the lessons from the said times.

10. **Spirit of Jealousy & Envy** - This spirit manifested in Heaven when Satan envied God's glory, and through jealousy, sought to obtain it! Jealously and envy are the dynamic duo which seem to reside secretly in the hearts of man until the time of aggravation has fully come. When left unchecked, this spirit opens the door for other spirits such as fear, vengeance, greed as well as confusion. Jealously and envy are manifested through withholding or stifling opportunities for others, burning desire to see what others have in your possession as well as rage or

irritation when you see a person with what you desire. (Proverbs 27:4)

Prayer Strategy: Command that spirit to be submitted to the Spirit of the Lord and cast to the pit of Hell. Invite the Holy Spirit into your life so that He can soothe the underlying pain and abandonment within your soul.

11. **Familiar Spirits** – Mentioned throughout scripture, these spirits have been identified as demonic agents masquerading as voices of light. These demonic spirits will sow seeds of discord and lies to misdirect people and cause them to sin. Familiar spirits manifest after family members have died, in dreams and visions as friends and colleagues as well as old habits designed as golden opportunities. (Acts 16:16 – 18)

Prayer Strategy: Command them to leave and do not return in Jesus' name. Also, render all of their words and sayings powerless by the authority of God. Bind up all workers of obeah's hands from evil works as such against you and your family the mighty name of Jesus Christ.

12. **Territorial Spirits** – These spirits are principalities that lord over regions and govern their spiritual flow. If the Lord God is not exalted in the region, the territorial spirits will intently and intensely fight against the saints. Once identified, territorial spirits can be dethroned and evicted through prayer and fasting. They are manifested through the common spiritual ills seen among the people, hindered prayers and unusual attacks on Christians. (Daniel 3:10 – 13)

Prayer Strategy: Ask the Lord to reveal to you what kind of principality is over your region then dethroned by cursing its roots of operation in the region. After persistently dismantling its cohort, cast all of its agent in the Abyss in Jesus' name. Most importantly, exalt the Spirit of the Lord over the region through intimate worship and praise.

13. **Ancestral Spirits** – these demonic spirits are normally invited into family bloodlines by the act of witchcraft and black magic. These spirits are contracted, knowingly and unknowingly, to fulfill a specific purpose such as providing resources, healing and even prosperity for the family or a particular sect within one. Once the request is granted then the spirits slowly gain access to souls within that bloodline using a string of similar spiritual hang-ups. This is also how generational curses are formed. (Deuteronomy 18:10 – 11)

Prayer Strategy: Repent on behalf of your previous generations and ask the Lord to be exalted as the only true and living God of your bloodline. Evict any spirits seeking refuge in your home and seal off any potential access points for their reentry. Also, break the cycles of sin from your generations to come in Jesus' name.

14. **Sorcery/Witchcraft** – the practice of evil works and spells have been going on for centuries, and there are people who use these dark arts to hurt and hinder others based on their personal desires. As believers, we must not fall for these devices or allow them to operate freely within our lives. You can tell that these acts are being performed against you based on your dreams and visions, the unusual sensations that you will feel (almost similar to being pricked by pins and needles) as well as being thrusted in confused state. (Galatians 5:16 – 20)

Prayer Strategy: Command the works of darkness to be exposed by the light of Jesus Christ. Decree and declare that their operations shall bring confusion upon their own camp. Cover yourself and your household under the blood of Jesus Christ. Above all else, ask the Lord to send angels on your behalf and defend you whenever your name is brought up in dark meetings.

15. **Succubus (Male) & Incubus (Female)** – This is a demonic agent goes throughout the spirit realm and attempts to have sexual encounters with targeted individuals. If one finds himself or herself having sexual relations of any kind in his or her dreams, he or she is actually having intercourse with a demon. The aftermath of such encounters is designed to bring afflictions upon the individual in the forms of sinus like symptoms, nausea and even migraines. Moreover, the main purpose of this demonically induced act is to transfer witchcraft and manipulated thoughts into the heart and mind of the individual. If someone found that he or she ejaculated or

climaxed during such an encounter, it would be incumbent of him or her to pray using the strategy below. On the other hand, if someone is raped or molested in his or her dreams, this is one of the beginning stages of demonic oppression. You would combat this kind of warfare through fasting and prayer. (Deuteronomy 23:9 – 11)

Prayer Strategy: Severe the soul tie and spiritual marriage in the name of Jesus Christ and plead the blood over your spiritual and natural body. Command all doors and points of contact that give these spirits access to your life to be sealed off and shut down in Jesus' name.

YOUR PERSONAL
JOURNAL

About the Author

Kenneth A. Miller is an apostle, author, global influencer and mentor. Upon receiving the call to ministry from the Lord in 2013, he embarked on a journey to spiritually transform the Bahamas as well as the world through the Truth of God's Word. He later accepted the Pastoral Call in 2015 and started a mission named 'New Zion Global Tabernacle' in one of the classrooms of the West End Primary School. This mission impacted the community and brought hope to the young people who visited the services. As 2016 drew near, the Lord commissioned him to establish Modern Day Exodus Global Church in the Downtown

Freeport district. On February 16th, 2017, after plowing for one year, he was ordained and licensed as a Minister of the Gospel and recognized nationally as an Apostle of the Lord Jesus Christ by Dr. Sidney McIntosh Sr.

As Apostle Miller continued pioneering in his ministerial career, the Lord granted Him the opportunity to receive various appointments by The Government of The Bahamas. On October 25th, 2017, he was appointed and sworn in as one of the youngest Justices of the Peace in the Commonwealth of The Bahamas. A few months later he received the appointment of Marriage Officer.

Recently, he authored and published several books including: *Manna Devotions: A Forty Day Devotional Book*, *The Faith Walk: Practical Ministry Tools for You* and *Saved, Single & Sexually Sound: A Thirty Day Devotional for You*. To this day, Apostle Kenneth A. Miller spends his time travelling to various islands and countries ministering the Gospel. He accredits all of his accomplishments as well as accolades to the Lord.

Other Products by the Author

Manna Devotional: A Forty Day Devotional:
Contained within the pages of *Manna Devotions: A Forty Day Devotional* are decrees and declarations which will strategically shift your life back into alignment with God's Perfect Will! Also readily available to you are journaling pages to document your most intimate prayers and growth in the Lord! *Manna Devotions: A Forty Day Devotional* is designed to strengthen you as you walk out of your wilderness into the blessings of God!

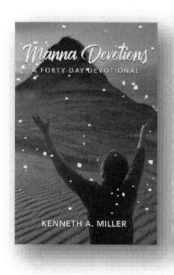

The Faith Walk: Practical Ministry Tools for You: Preparing and equipping the next generation of spiritual leaders is the main focus of *The Faith Walk: Practical Ministry Tools for You*. This book, designed with a textbook element, acts as a biblical leadership development program. Above all else, this book pushes the individual out of his/her comfort zone into the position of power God has ordained for his/her life.

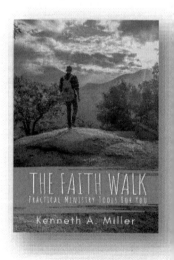

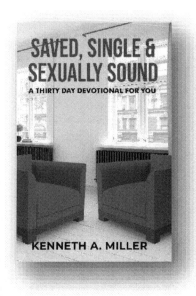

Saved, Single & Sexually Sound: A Thirty Day Devotional for You: Singlehood is an adventurous time of one's life, but it can be filled with many challenges. *Saved, Single & Sexually Sound: A Thirty Day Devotional for You* is here to help you navigate through the tussles of being saved and single while remaining sexually pure before the Lord. Equipped with journal pages, you are able to pen daily your intimate feelings and prayers as you encourage yourself in the beauty of singlehood!

A Letter to the Watchman: Today's Heart to Heart with God: There is a sound of hope and encouragement coming forth from Heaven to empower the end time leaders! *A Letter to the Watchman: Today's Heart to Heart with God* has been ordained to strengthen your resolve as you traverse the land ministering the Gospel. Equipped with a journaling section and a strategic fasting regimen, this book equips you with the necessary tools to overthrow the

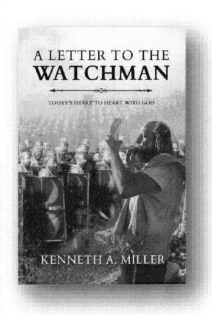

plans of the satanic forces in your region. You are God's watchman, and it is time for your heart to heart with Him today!

Authorship: Strategies for Writing and Self-Publishing: There is a group of people called by God to write words that will influence and empower generations to come. These individuals have also been endowed with supernatural wisdom and the scribal anointing. Therefore, Authorship: Strategies for Writing and Self-Publishing has been birthed to equip uprising authors with the necessary tools to articulate the thoughts placed on their hearts on paper. Designed with a course outline and step by step teachings, this book will strengthen you in the art of authorship.

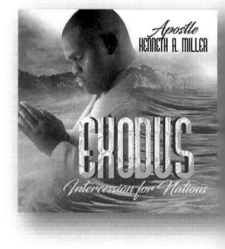

Exodus: Intercession for Nations: In every generation, there is a stirring in the hearts of those called to lift up prayers on behalf of their nation. Found on major digital media outlets, *Exodus: Intercession for Nations* is a prayer CD dedicated to equipping the next generation of intercessors with the strategies to overthrow demonic agencies and principalities which lord over their region spiritually. Just as Moses lead a people out of bondage with power packed prayers so shall you in this present age!

Made in the USA
Columbia, SC
27 September 2024

42392765R00057